C000081376

Stark Raving Dad

Stark Raving Dad

POEMS FOR THE ~~LOVING~~ FRAZZLED PARENT IN ALL OF US

RUNNING PRESS
PHILADELPHIA

Copyright © 2019 by Sanderson Dean

Hachette Book Group supports the right to free expression
and the value of copyright. The purpose of copyright is
to encourage writers and artists to produce the creative
works that enrich our culture.

The scanning, uploading, and distribution of this book
without permission is a theft of the author's intellectual
property. If you would like permission to use material
from the book (other than for review purposes), please
contact permissions@hbgusa.com. Thank you for your support
of the author's rights.

Running Press
Hachette Book Group
1290 Avenue of the Americas, New York, NY 10104
www.runningpress.com
@Running_Press

First Edition: May 2019

Published by Running Press, an imprint of Perseus Books,
LLC, a subsidiary of Hachette Book Group, Inc.

The Hachette Speakers Bureau provides a wide range of
authors for speaking events. To find out more, go to
www.hachettespeakersbureau.com or call (866) 376-6591.

The publisher is not responsible for websites (or their
content) that are not owned by the publisher.

Print book design by Rachel Peckman.

Library of Congress Control Number: 2018955313

ISBNs: 978-0-7624-9360-9 (hardcover), 978-0-7624-9359-3
(ebook)

RRD-S

10 9 8 7 6 5 4 3 2 1

Dedicated to my two boys,
Jordan and Kylan.

Thanks for all the inspiration.

CONTENTS

Dear Dad,

Fatherhood is an amazing adventure. Unfortunately, by the fourth sleepless night, you probably won't remember any of it. Suddenly you'll have a lot on your hands — like germs, spit-up, and probably snot. Only a strong sense of self-preservation can get you through. That, and conveniently overlooking loaded diapers.

Sadly, kids don't come with instructions — and frankly, we probably wouldn't read them anyway. In my case, the kids wouldn't sleep. They wouldn't eat. They wouldn't stop crying. They kept making messes. And they *still* don't flush the toilet. (Sound familiar?)

After years of listening to my whining, my wife challenged me to do something more constructive with my angst. And now you're reading it! Everything here is based on real life, real joy, and real torment. Even the artwork is real — compliments of my kids.

Inspiration came one afternoon while plunging a toilet...for the second time that day. When I shared "Ode to the Plungerman" with my family, it was an instant hit. Apparently, everyone loves to laugh at Dad's pain. Now, after more than four years of capturing all my experiences in the form of poems, I feel like it's time to share my bitter, cathartic humor with all the other Stark Raving Dads out there. Misery loves company, and let's face it: you're not the only frazzled parent picking Craisins out of your couch cushions.

Welcome to the club,
Your Fellow Frazzled Dad

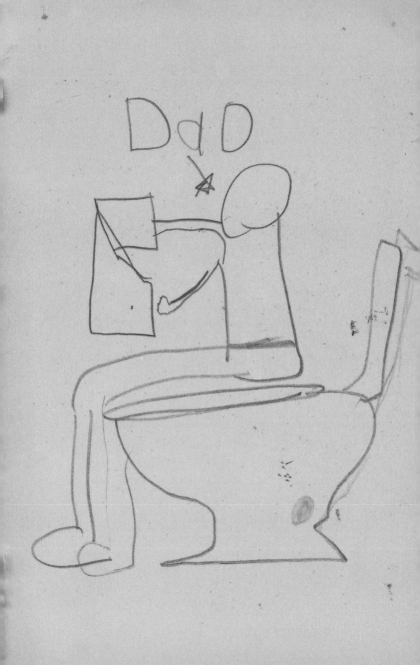

CHAPTER 1:

TAKING TIME FOR YOURSELF
& OTHER MYTHS

Okay, so you're a parent. Now what? There's
no manual. There's no do-overs. And there's
definitely no breaks. These are poems about
those quiet times...when Dad realizes
there's also no escape.

Go with the flow.
But keep your plunger handy.

Stark Raving Dad (Adage)

ARE YOU LISTENING?

My wife finally made her point
It took forever

She —
No you can't have that
Said — .
What are you guys getting into?
That —
Stop hitting your brother
I —
Wait, is that gum?
Need —
I'll help you in a second
To —
Give me the stick
Listen —
Where'd you get that?
Better

LOVING HANDS

Always grabbing
Always clinging
Always sticking

Where have they been?
What have they touched?
When were they clean?

Now they're here
Rubbing my face
Your hands letting me know
We share everything
Like your runny nose

KING FOR
A MINUTE

Here I sit upon the throne
How I wish I was alone
First comes one kid, then the cat
Then comes pounding
What was that?

It used to be a quiet time
A place of solace, not a crime
No one questioning whilst I sat
Now everyone's wondering
Where I'm at

I miss the past, when mine was mine
Including all my bathroom time
More frantic knocking
C'mon, what's wrong?
I mumble that I won't be long

LOVE & PUKE

Warm and wet
I hear the splatter
But I'm too numb
For it to matter
Liquid spreads across my chest
Drips that haven't come to rest
I wipe your tears
I share your sighs
Two weary souls
With muffled cries
Plaintive eyes and burning head
Abandon thoughts of sleep and bed

No more wondering if you're sick
I hug you close
And feel us stick

16

THE DIAPER AISLE

I stare

Lost in the glare

Of bright, fluorescent light

So many options, so many offers
So many pitfalls late at night

So many sizes, so many styles
So many selections to get right

So many categories, so many colors
So many covers to compute

So many containers, so many catchers
So many collectors — for poop

THE PROBLEM SOLVER

The future looks up at me
With a hopeful smile
And the question sits

The charge of parental duty
For more rainbow sprinkles
Or temper fits

These choices in life
Define us
And tension mounts

These tests of resolve
Shape us
And seconds count

The moment tense
I can't be wrong
My decision swift —
Go ask Mom

SUNDAY MORNING
WAKE-UP CALL

A footstep
A giggle
A jump on the bed
A moan
A crash
A thump in the head

A scream
A bark
A cereal spill
A fight
A bite
A threat to kill

A screech
A curse
A bang on the wall
A grumble
A groan
Arise —
To your Sunday morning wake-up call

THE FIRST POOP

Who could imagine I'd be so proud
Floating, joyous, upon a cloud
A little grunt
A soft kerflop
One small floatie that pleases Pop

In beaming eyes, I see the glow
A toilet triumph, your best-in-show
The drop in the bucket
The beginning of the end
Call out the heralds
Ring all of our friends

No diaper change
No stinky mess
This poop's on target
Our greatest success

Potty-trained forevermore!
Until...you lose focus
In aisle eight of the hardware store

I Wiht to Get a I
Pet FISH

FISH FLUSH

I never thought I'd do it
I never thought I'd lie
But I'm staring at a third fish
That had to go and die

Tears, moans, wails, and whoa
Gaze up in clouded eyes
A ruse to dodge a little grief
Should come as no surprise

A fish is a fish and a flush is a flush
So off to the store I go
And when I return with a new Mr. Bubbles
No one will ever know

CHAPTER 2:

SLEEP & OTHER THINGS YOU'LL NEVER ENJOY AGAIN

There comes a point in every dad's life when he realizes he no longer has a life. Don't expect time for sleep, brushing your teeth, or barbecues. These poems are about finding your happy place — then kissing it goodbye.

Responsibility arrives
upon the winds of diaper change.

Stark Raving Dad (Proverb)

RELAX & IGNORE
THE TOOTHPASTE

Standing here
Quiet
Moments after bedtime
Breathe deep
This is your time to think
Ignore the toothpaste
On the edge of the sink
And the mirror
And the floor
And the wall
And the door

THE TUCKING PROCESS

I tuck you in —
Because it's bedtime
Then —
Because you heard a noise
Next —
Because you're thirsty
Shortly —
Because you had a question
Later —
Because you're not tired
Again —
Because it's too hot
After that —
Because you had a bad dream
Even though you haven't slept
Finally —
I tuck you in next to Mom
So I can sleep on the couch

A DATE
WITH MOM

The lights dim
The wine pours
The music plays
The candle flickers

Eyes lock
Hands touch
Senses tingle
Heads lean together

Softly
. You whisper to me:
Did we leave enough diapers?

ME, MYSELF & PEE

At the weary hour of three
I ponder
Liquid impossibility

Bleary eyes that strain to see
The wonder
Of Ultra Absorbency

But proof lies in front of me
Your diaper
No miracle-sponge anomaly

Naked now, you set truth free
Revealing
My shirt too — can soak up pee

FLOATIE IN
THE TUB

I pooped! I pooped!
I see, I see
It's there
Floating in the tub

You smile
I smile
As we ponder your circling sub

No pain
All contained
I'm far beyond reacting

On this, we can all agree
A bath is so relaxing

ALL THE RICHES
IN THE WORLD

Gold
Diamonds
Riches
Rubies
Fame
Fortune
Cash
Caviar
Champagne
Gems
Limousines
Private jets
Islands
Life
The universe
Anything
Everything
I'd give it all —
For sleep

32

ALMOST PURE

Sweltering sun
On city street
Sharing a drink
To beat the heat

Just a sip
Clean and refreshing
My bottled water
A liquid blessing

Now orange speckles
Swirl within
Lazily floating
For me to dive in

Changing my mind
I realize I'm done
There's only enough
Goldfish-cracker water for one

DON'T PLAY
IN LINE

STUCK IN THE
EVER-MOVING LINE

Stuck in line
It begins...

Fidgeting
Fiddling
Wriggling
Jiggling
Squirming
Turning
Twisting
Tugging
Jerking
Jolting
Thumping
Bumping
Swinging
Flinging
Flopping
Grasping
Grabbing
Wait —
I have my phone

And by its magical light
You turn to stone

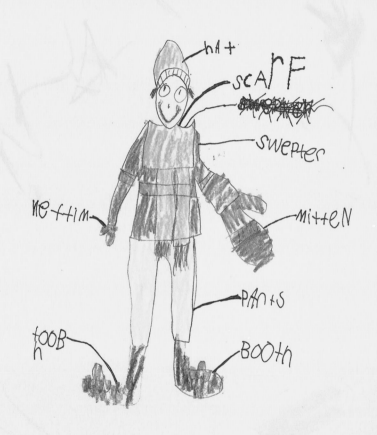

hat

scARF

~~scarf~~

swepter

nettim

mitteN

PANts

tooB
n

BOOth

BUNDLED FOR THE WINTER

Thick socks. Long underwear.
    Warm sweater.
Stay still.
This is better.
Snow pants. Coat. Hat.
Stand up.
Stop that.
Boots. Mittens. Fingers all crunched.
Let's try this again, wait...
Your socks are bunched?
Take off your boots.
We may never leave.
What's wrong with your sleeve?
I'll fix your scarf.
We've got to rewrap it.
And we're still trying
    to zip up your jacket.
Yes —
I know it's hot,
But outside it's not.
We're taking great care,
Making sure you're prepared.
And now...

You have to go potty?

CHAPTER 3:

YELLING & OTHER THINGS
THAT DON'T WORK

For every action there is a reaction, and
however you react, you're wrong. Sorry,
Dad. Did we mention there's no training
manual? Yeah, these are poems about that.

Don't waste your time wondering
if you're doing everything right.
You aren't.

Stark Raving Dad (Maxim)

40

NO ONE
IGNORES ME BETTER

I say your name, softly at first
Then louder, with more authority

Firmer, like a school teacher
Commanding, like a police officer
Barking, like a drill sergeant
Shouting, like a stock trader
Roaring, like a football coach
Screaming, like a rabid fan
Finally,
YELLING
Like a dad

And still,
Somehow —
You don't hear me

NO TISSUE
TO THE RESCUE

Like lava
Like time
Unstoppable
The snot dripping from your nose

No tissue
No wipes
Unwatchable
The slime dangling toward your toes

Stay calm
Stay cool
Unflappable
We've got places to go

One sleeve
One swipe
Unshakable
Roll it up like a parenting pro

THE DARKSIDE
DISPOSAL

Panic
No time to think
Stop it! Stop it! Stop it!!
Breathlessly
Staring at the sink
Whatever it is, we lost it

Pondering
That terrible sound
Imagining
Those items ground

Spoons, lids
Tupperware
Beaten and mangled
Beyond repair

Reaching in
To find instead
Darth Vader
Minus a head

43

ROAD TRIP CONCIERGE

Welcome to the passenger side
Just remember
You're not along for the ride

You're the concierge
Constantly attending, fixing
And wiping up
Contorting your body
To get things unstuck
Dropped toys, treats, sporks, and spills
Crayons, nuggets, napkins, and refills

Even a movie
Can't stop this barrage
The end of the journey
A distant mirage

Eyes burn into me, when you realize
Long before we arrive —
You should have asked to drive

HATE BEFORE SCHOOL

Hate lives in angry eyes
Hate knows disdainful sighs
Hate walks with us to school
Hate's scorn, irrefutable

Hate follows a darkened path
Hate stews in growing wrath
Hate is eternal, hate never stops
Hate just glares, with a lunch box

Hate will say no goodbye
Hate will silence my reply
Hate is a cold sneer as you go
All because you wanted an Oreo

THREATS

Staring at their faces
I know it better be good
Threats don't always work
Even though they should

My glares will scare
My words will astound
My volume will rise
I'm not messing around

Timeout is soft
Naptime is weak
It's got to be something
That doesn't sound meek

I want them to know
I'm nobody's stooge
My wrath should be epic,
Unforgettable, huge

The Earth will tremble
The mountains will rock
Is a year without food too much?
Just to pick up a sock

CLEAN UP YOUR ROOM

Clean up your room
Clean up your room
Clean up your room
Clean up your room
Clean up your room
Clean up your room
Clean up your room
Clean up your room
How many times do I have to say it?

47

48

THE SPACE
ON YOUR HEAD

Something's not right
Something's amiss
On your face
I sense an emptiness

Something's not right
As I contemplate
Your strange smile
Makes me hesitate

Something's not right
Was it something I said?
Then I notice
The space on your head

Something's not right
Now I'm fully aware
Beaming pride obvious
You cut your own hair!

COOKIES 'N' CRIME

Guilty
You condemn
Guilty
By pointed finger

Our cookie culprit caught this time
Don't let the mystery linger
Your brother can't refute the crime
Trust your pointed finger

Guilty
Say your chocolate lips
Guilty
By pointed finger

Earnest with obvious lie
Crumbs reveal the ringer
But you're confident there's no alibi —
For a pointed finger

CHAPTER 4:

PLAYTIME & OTHER MESS- MAKING ADVENTURES

When toys cover the ground like snow and food coats every other surface, it's time for the kids to start a new project! Usually with gallons of glue and a bazillion broken crayons. This is a little poetic homage to all the games and activities that make *more* work for Dad.

Even if you've seen it all— you'll never see it coming.

Stark Raving Dad (Tenet)

THE MASTERPIECE

All that cutting
And meticulous care
Glue
Just the right shapes
In just the right places
Glue
The utmost concentration
The required contemplation
Glue
You step away
Your masterwork through

And your priceless art
Perfectly stuck
To the kitchen table

THE MEASURE OF
A TAPE MEASURE

You created your own universe
Inch by inch
A simple tool —
Pulled to epic lengths
Twisted to brave frontiers

The walls of a fort
The boundaries of a space station
The edges of imagination
And finally —
The distance of irritation

Stretched to max length
Fifty feet of calculated fun
Woven around fences,
Bushes,
Bicycles,
Chairs,
Railings,
Trees,

Tables,
Spickets,
Posts,
Flower pots,
Tomato plants,
Wheel barrows,
And barbecue grill handles

The only thing it can't measure —
Is Dad's patience
It extends far beyond that

I like ot whrk
with toos
I like to
make lots
of sof

I like to. PLAYGUN

58

THE LIFE OF
A SQUIRT GUN

Bright colors, now faded
Resting quietly on the lawn
How soon the joys of summer
Have come and gone

Full of life and laughs
Just days before
Now, abandoned weapons
That don't squirt anymore

Cracked, empty plastic
Leaking the fun
Can't take the pressure
Of boys on the run

Dropped without sadness
When you're on the go
Waiting for Dad to move them —
So he can mow

KIDS SHOULD NEVER HAVE SHARPIES

Kids should never have Sharpies
Even if you appreciate wall art

Kids should never have Sharpies
Even if you like stick figures
On your coffee table

Kids should never have Sharpies
Even if you're cool
With neck tattoos

Kids should never have Sharpies
Even if you like to wash them
With your clothes

Seriously, permanent is forever
And Dad isn't laughing at that mustache
    anymore

DIRECTIONS FOR KICKING A BALL

There's only one way to kick a ball
And that's really, really hard

If you want to smash it far
Kick it really, really hard

If you want to blast it high
Kick it really, really hard

If you kick a ball at all
Kick it really, really hard

But you probably should have listened
When Dad told you to kick it in the yard

Because that lamp is really, really
    broken

BOYS & STICKS

There's nothing better
Than a stick
A few feet long
But not too thick

Something to poke
Something to swing
A powerful weapon
To rule as a king

No fancy game
You can buy at the store
No flashy gadget
That costs a lot more

If you were smart, Dad
And a little more swift
You'd wrap *this* up
As a birthday gift

QUALITY TIME

Is six hours
Putting together a Lego space station
Really fine?
Can we still call it
Quality time?

I haven't seen anyone in forever
Digging through tiny pieces
Alone

Glaring at bits of plastic
Lost

A pile of torture
Daring me to realize
We're only halfway done

And suddenly
Here you are
Telling me — Mom's a lot more fun

THE PICK

Finger in nose
I saw you pick it
Now you're wondering
Where to stick it
Hand...slowly...drifting
Toward the couch
But then —
You flick it

BRUISES & BUMPS

I've seen bruises
And I've seen bumps
I've seen scratches
And I've seen lumps
I've seen stitches
And I've seen spills
I've seen doctors
And I've seen bills
But what is brotherly love —
If it doesn't come with a shove?

THE HARDEST THING
IN THE WORLD

If you've ever stepped
On a small, square block
In the dark at two o'clock
It's more than a shock
It's harder than rock
Your jaw will lock
To stifle the scream, and whimper
instead
Why did I get out of bed?

Emblazoned brightly with an "A"
Nestled near an apple
Impassionedly I have to say
It really hurts like crapple

CHAPTER 5:

SANITY & OTHER THINGS
GOING DOWN THE TOILET

These poems delve into the things that
drive Dad *insane*! He'd write more, but he
needs to turn off every light in the house,
pick up dirty socks in the front yard, then
get the plunger...again.

Be the bigger person.
Using your size and weight
is a huge advantage.

            Stark Raving Dad (Truism)

ODE TO THE
PLUNGER MAN

Dear Dad,
You're always there
When something's stuck
Be it Q-tips
Or a Dixie cup

Our hero fighting crayons in muck
More enemies rising as it fills up

Army men, a rubber gator,
Bouncy balls, the Caped Crusader
The only constant
In this stopped-up crater?
Half a roll of toilet paper

With a gurgle of greatness
Then a mighty lunge
Triumphant!
You make your final plunge

ROAD-TRAPPED

Help
We're trapped in a car
An hour travelled
And we've gone too far

A quiet ride
Lost in the past
Praying for an end
Now driving too fast

Tortured by tantrums
Splattered by spills
Seatbelt prisoners
Losing our wills

Can we survive
This titanic task?
Our road-trip vacation...
At long last

ALWAYS DRY YOUR ROCKS

Always dry your rocks
Just listen for the knocks
Washing, spinning, every one
When Mom shouts
You'll know they're done

In the dryer, warm and waiting
Silent after clanging, banging
And once she frantically stops it —
You can put them back in your pocket

LAMENT OF THE KNOTTED SHOELACES

Your intricate knot
A sinister plot
To test a father's skill
Twists upon turns
Tangled and mangled
Devised to break my will

Contorted fingers, bent to the fight
Brow furrowed, pulling with might
Feeling the heat
The clock is ticking
Sweating through shirt
Your laces constricting

But I'm the one who let you choose
Stating proudly, you can tie your shoes
Now we're late
We need to go
My lesson learned —

Stick with Velcro

PRESSING DAD'S BUTTONS

Crackers become crumbs
Clickety-clack
Crumbs become crushed
Clackety-click
Crushed becomes crud
Tippity-tap
Crud becomes crammed
Tappity-tip

Crushed cracker crumb crud
Mixed with drool, made with ease
Crammed into all my computer keys

That's how you press Dad's buttons

THE CALM BEFORE
THE SMELL

Behind the wheel
I savor the calm
One perfect moment
When nothing is wrong

But look again
That grimace is telling
Use your senses
That's horror you're smelling

Trouble onboard
And there's no escape
Trapped in a car
Reaching panic state

Voices rising
Mom even nagged
How could you forget —

The diaper bag?!

I HEAR
EVERYTHING YOU SAY

I hear everything you say
If I want to
Otherwise you're talking to yourself
Or yelling for no reason
Or just turning red

By the way
I heard you whispering to Mom
Through four walls
Fifty feet away
When I was supposed to be sleeping
    in bed

SCAMPERING SOCKS

Dirty socks
Lounge on the floor

Dirty socks
Hide behind doors

Dirty socks
Loaf on the stairs

Dirty socks
Hang off chairs

But dirty socks scamper
When you look in the hamper —
Because you never find dirty socks there

82

TURBULENCE IN 13B

The thrill of flying
Thump!
The love of airplanes
Thump! Thump!
The joy of travel
Thump!
The wonder of tray tables
Thump! Thump!
The marvel of tight spaces
Thump!
The grimace from Seat 13B
Thump! Thump!
Let's call it turbulence
Thump!

My family is _____ ing.

GETTING OUT THE DOOR

The biggest problem
With going to the store
Is actually getting out the door

Do we really need snacks
And the mighty Thor?
Do we need that rubber snake
And those weapons of war?

Then, we're loading, strapping,
Prepping for snags
Packing tissues, wipes,
And the diaper bag

Finally, we make our arrival
An epic journey of survival
But there's one thing we missed —

The list

CHAPTER 6:

FOOD & OTHER THINGS KIDS DON'T EAT

Like a teething biscuit mashed into your computer keyboard, food rarely ends up where it should. Parents constantly battle spills, sticky fingers, and picky eaters. But not eating French fries?! C'mon!

Some things are just easier... when you ignore them.

Stark Raving Dad (Aphorism)

SERVED BETWEEN
YOUR TOES

There's just something
About noodles on the floor
Squishing between your toes
As you walk through the door

A rubbery-wet texture
Grimy, slick, and turning gray
My compliments to the chef —
They feel *al dente*

BETTER BUTTER

Open the lid and behold the treasure
A golden spread of past meals' pleasure

Flashes of crimson
Streaks of brown
Bits of flavor, all around

Like muffin crumbs, jelly
And grated cheddar
All making our butter
So much better

First bread
then Jelly
then eat it

WHERE PEANUT BUTTER GOES

Peanut butter
Goes great on sandwiches
Cabinets, counters
And refrigerator doors

Peanut butter
Goes great on toast
Chairs, doorknobs
And smeared on floors

Peanut butter
Goes great on crackers
Coffee makers, couches
And carpeting

Honestly —
Peanut butter goes great
On everything

And so does jelly

MANNERS BY
THE MOUTHFUL

It's no big deal
Talking with your mouth full

It's just a meal
Malfing wiff yorsh mouff flll

It's just Dad always getting mad
Talshing weff yrrff mouff flll

It's just food in the way
When you've got things to say
Talshnng wrsh yurr mouff ffllll

It's just a small amount
Sometimes slipping out
Dalshnng wrrf yrrr mrff fffll

At least the dog doesn't mind
Talking with your mouth full

FEEDING TIME

Staring at my plate again
Wishing I could eat
Wiping up milk that's spilled —
And dripping in my seat

Followed by refills
Spooning out orders
Washing kids' faces
And serving as porter

Now there's no time
So I'm cramming food down
I'm told to stop dawdling —
And ditch the frown

WASTE NOT,
WANT NO MORE

I am going to drink this milk
Because we're at a restaurant
And I paid five bucks

I am going to drink this milk
Because I'm tired of waste
And I'm ending the squander

I am going to drink this milk
And the half-eaten surprise
Hidden at the bottom

But next time —
I'm not going to drink your
Leftover milk

EVIL, EVIL BROCCOLI

You just sit and glare at me
Between us both
Evil, evil broccoli

Warm, healthy veggies to eat
Silent, waiting there
Evil, evil broccoli

A line drawn with a timeless foe
Staring back
Evil, evil broccoli

Once leafy, green, and oh-so-good
But an hour later, you taste like wood
Evil, evil broccoli

Just scrape it in the sink
Don't tell Mom
Evil, evil broccoli

THE ICING
ON THE FACE

Blue hands
Blue lips
Blue face

Blue icing all over the place

What could be better than frosting?
Certainly not cake
Cause you haven't touched a lick of it

STICKING TOGETHER

Gripping and grabbing
With glistening gunk
Coating our fingers
In layers of funk

Dripping your excess
Inside the fridge
Crust-over-leakage
On half-screwed lids

Mustard, ketchup, steak sauce
And dressing
Doors open wide
While kids are assessing

Small hands work hard
When we open containers
So, stick with us, Dad —
No one likes a complainer

ICE CREAM SCREAMS

I scream
You scream
We all scream
For ice cream
But Dad screams the loudest
When he's cleaning it
Off his new teak chairs

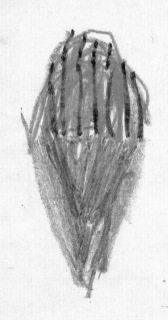

THIS ISN'T A RESTAURANT

You order French fries
You order a chocolate shake
You order another milk
And a grilled cheese

But there's no menu
No chef
No waiter
And no maître d'

So finish your meatloaf
Get your own milk
And take three bites
Of your broccoli

You're not in a restaurant
You don't have broken knees
And even worse —
You didn't say *please*

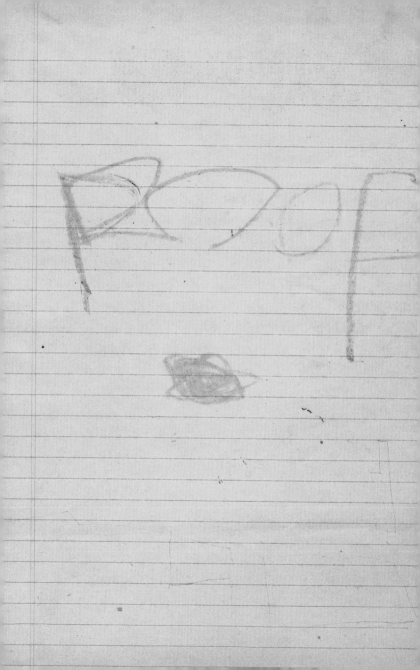

CHAPTER 7:

STOP & SMELL
THE...UH-OH

No matter what you see, you'll never see it
coming. Don't say we didn't warn you. These
are poems about life's little surprises.
They usually flow downhill, toward Dad.

That's not a dirty diaper —
that's the smell of duty.

Stark Raving Dad (Axiom)

MOM'S HOME

Mom's home! Mom's home!
Who's more excited
Kids, dog, or Dad?

Mom's home! Mom's home!
Her clean, tidy house
Now trashed and sad

Mom's home! Mom's home!
Stains on the carpet
Don't look so bad

Mom's home! Mom's home!
Her loving eyes glitter
Hiding the mad

Mom's home! Mom's home!
And Dad just realized —
He shouldn't be glad

THE DISTANT GIGGLE

A giggle together
Can brighten the world
Warming my heart, my spirit unfurled
But giggles in the distance
When I'm not around
Are rarely the same, comforting sound

What could be joyful
Behind those closed doors?
I doubt it will take me
To happier shores

I'm suddenly dreading
All the stickers and glue
My coveted phone, no longer in view

STICKY-BROWN STAINS

Screams
Blasphemy
Worse

Gnashing
Snarling
Curse

Eyes on fire
Reaching into dryer
And finding
Warm, fresh horror

Victims of a Tootsie Roll

DEEP IN THE CUSHIONS

On the arm of the couch
Cheese-dust fingerprints

Beyond a trail of animal-cracker crumbs
Craisins

Across the dimpled seat
Pretzel pieces

Reaching deep into the cushions —
Something wet

HIDDEN EVIDENCE

Behind your dresser is a darkened lair
A crime scene soiled in twisted pairs
Mom and Dad so unaware
Gasping now at underwear

A sour grimace, noting the smell
It did seem sudden —
That you were potty-trained so well

WHY ARE WE LATE?

Why are we late?
You always ask
Is it because we can't find our shoes?

Why are we late?
You always wonder
Is it because we're missing our jacket?

Why are we late?
You always moan
Is it because we forgot our lunch?

Why are we late?
You always fume
Is it because we have to go pee?

Why are we late?
You always whine
Well, I'll tell you, Dad —
It's because school starts too early

BRIGHT-EYED & FLUFFY

Oh-so-adorable, bright-eyed and fluffy
We've got to have
This cute little puppy

The kids will love him
Won't it be great?
This wagging joy, the perfect playmate

A trusty companion you just can't deny
So I force a smile and swallow my reply

To me, it sounds like more poop
And Dad's the one —
Left holding the scoop

CAR SEAT CLEANING

What hides in the creases?
What waits in the folds?
What sticks on the straps?
What lurks in the holes?

What horror could this be
Coating the buckles?
What filth have I found
Smeared on my knuckles?

What evil is looming
The more I clean deep?
What kind of parent
Locks a kid into this seat?

THE UNFLUSHED HAIKU

In the bowl, I float
Serene upon the water
Why don't you flush me?

CHAPTER 8:

STILL STANDING! LIKE THE WALKING DEAD

If you've made it this
far...congratulations! You may survive
parenthood, after all. These are poems
about Dad's little triumphs and not-total-
failures. Like the quiet thrill of picking
up dog poop — far away from screaming kids.

Sometimes,
the best way to clean a room —
is to shut the door.

Stark Raving Dad (Dictum)

YELLING FOR FUN

Everybody loves to yell
It lets out stress
It gets you pumped
It channels your emotion
It hits a high note
It demands a response
And it gets the best attention
When Dad's on a conference call

MY BEST FRIEND

So still
So quiet
So peaceful

Find companionship in his light
Find calm in his control
Find comfort in his glow

His charm is my best friend
His beauty comes from within
His name is Television

Does he challenge minds? No.
He channels mercy

SNARFLING IN
THE LIVING ROOM

What's in that corner
Where there shouldn't be food?
Licking, slobbering, snarfling
Yet, quietly subdued

Slumped on the couch, it's only just me
A chance to relax and watch some TV
Ignoring this mystery can't be so wrong
Whatever it is, it will soon be gone

So eat up, my furry friend
And enjoy my reticence
Just make sure —
You erase all the kids' evidence

THE DELICATE DROP-OFF

Sometimes...
You just need a break

Sometimes...
You just want a moment

Sometimes...
You just seek an escape

Sometimes...
You covertly drop the kid at daycare
With a loaded diaper

THE MAGIC STRIP

Oh, the excitement. The joy.
The anticipation.
The fun. The wonder. The elation.
This plastic strip sensation
Fulfilling every expectation

Enchanted magic it yields
Just after peeled
From screaming and crying
To perfectly healed
Halting the pain
Ending the woe
Who would believe
You're ready to go

Forgetting all that panic you made
Until the next time...
You need a Band-Aid

MEETING THE PEDIATRICIAN

Before the first appointment
We met your new pediatrician
For a second time

A quiet nod
A knowing smile
With nothing said

Here again —
Removing stitches
From your head

A PIRANHA WITH A HORN

I said no to a cat
I said no to a dog
I said no to a hamster
I said no to a frog
But a piranha with a horn?
That's a possible pet
And as a selfless dad
I say, why not? Let's check

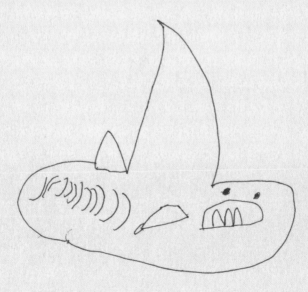

DAD'S QUIET TIME

How to find quiet time
Without the guilt
No reproachful stares
Making resolve wilt

I'm walking the dog
It has to be done
And with a little silence
It's almost fun

I can hear myself think
As I walk this loop
A smile on my face
As I pick up poop

ACKNOWLEDGMENTS

My deepest thanks to all my family and friends who became guinea pigs for my eccentric "pop poetry," and who were gracious enough to give gentle criticism and guidance. I also have to thank Jordana Tusman, Mark Gottlieb, and all the people at Running Press who actually gave the rantings of a frazzled dad their belief and effort. Most especially, I have to thank my wife, Lorna, who sat through countless revisions and readings of "poems" (some good, some remarkably awful). Without her support, you probably wouldn't be reading this. She also spent countless hours in the sweaty, dusty, thousand-degree attic, digging out our kids' "masterpieces." Lorna, your tireless help and constant belief has meant the world to me.

Finally, I want to thank my two boys, Jordan and Kylan. Obviously, without you, none of this would have been possible. I'm sure you know all my ravings are just that — ravings. I love you very much.

the
end